Clemson University Flag

Built of brick made from red clay of the Piedmont, the Clemson College Main Building contrasts the bright blue sky of upper South Carolina. The clock tower is accentuated by a sandstone frieze of ornate swirling flowers which fits like a collar above the face of the clock. Round arched windows rest on this frieze and provide a four sided 'reviewing stand' for the departed spirits of Tigers, said to sometimes revisit Clemson... This honored sentinel above Tillman Hall has been witness and guardian for the thousands of loyal sons and daughters of Tigertown whose lives have been enriched in its shadows.

Mary Catherine Littlejohn in *Tales of Tigertown*, 1979

Tillman Hall

CLEMSON
UNIVERSITY

Photographed by Seny Norasingh

HARMONY HOUSE
PUBLISHERS LOUISVILLE

Picture a large country estate of 1500 acres in the rolling foothills of the Blue Ridge Mountains with stately buildings placed at elevated points within an irregular circle. To the north and outlined against the sky is range after range of lofty mountains, in the summer clothed with verdure and standing out a deep blue against the horizon and often in winter with snow. Smooth roads and walks wind over and around the hills. Groves of large graceful oaks spread their great branches to make a cool, inviting shade on a summer day. Grassy slopes dotted here and there with beds of brilliant flowers all combine to make a campus famed for its beauty. This is the home of the Clemson Tigers.

From "Student Life at Clemson," 1921

John Carroll's painting of the first Board of Trustees meeting

Executive Editors: William Butler and William Strode
Library of Congress Catalog Number: 87-083178
Hardcover International Standard Book Number 0-916509-41-9
Printed in USA by Reynolds-Foley Company, Louisville, Kentucky
First Edition printed Fall, 1988 by Harmony House Publishers,
P.O. Box 90, Prospect, Kentucky 40059 (502) 228-2010 / 228-4446
Copyright © 1988 by Harmony House Publishers
Photographs Copyright © 1988 by Seny Norasingh

This book or portions thereof may not be reproduced in any form without permission of Harmony House Publishers. Photographs may not be reproduced in any form without permission of Seny Norasingh.

Statue of Thomas Green Clemson by A. Wolfe Davidson

"The Tiger" by A. Wolfe Davidson

Sikes Hall

FOREWORD

When I stepped onto the Clemson Agricultural College campus in September of 1929, it was a smaller place than it is today. The student cadet corps was less than one-sixth the size of today's student body. Our lives centered on the barracks, the parade ground, a few classroom buildings, the laboratories, and the agricultural fields. Many of the faculty and staff lived on campus. Those who did not, lived within easy walking distance of the campus. The little town had a few stores, a stable, and five churches. In many ways, it was the campus that the original trustees, the early presidents, those dedicated faculty, and the students would have known.

Time has its way, however, and in the near sixty years since I came, two themes have been constant. The first has been to preserve and protect our heritage — our tradition. So today, surviving from those earlier years, are the landmarks of Clemson University. Fort Hill House, the family home of the Calhouns and the Clemsons, remains the soul of this remarkable school. Like the Calhouns and the Clemsons before us, Clemson faculty, students, alumni, and staff seek solutions to today's challenges through the great missions of teaching, research, and service. Guarding the tradition and enhancing the vision are the monuments of the first century, including those landmarks I remember as a youth — Tillman, Sikes, and Hardin — which continue to be part of the heart of our University.

There are also the monuments that speak to Clemson's ability to cope with the challenges of the last 100 years and to look to the future. The vast array of dormitories that now have housed the 62,000 daughters and sons of dear old Clemson; the R. M. Cooper Library, the mind of the University, with its lighted windows that shine into the night; the array of classrooms, laboratories and recreational buildings and areas — these are part both of Clemson's tradition and the vision of the generations of Clemson's caretakers.

This book is a pictorial essay of that tradition — a tradition which itself is a vision. Over 100 years ago, Thomas Green Clemson had a vision. If only he could see it now! Nearly 60 years ago, I caught a glimpse of that vision as have many members of all the classes that have entered here.

This book captures a part of the physical and the human tradition of this great school, the inheritance that the first century passes on to the second. You cannot have a second century without the first. But without a vision of the second century, the first will vanish. Tradition and vision — they add up to Clemson.

Robert C. Edwards

Bowman Field

THIS SPECIAL PLACE CALLED CLEMSON

This special place called Clemson began life more than 100 years ago as Fort Hill. That was the name of the plantation and the home of John C. Calhoun, South Carolina's greatest statesman.

During his long career in public service, the Carolina-born and Yale-educated Calhoun served in the U.S. Senate, as Secretary of War and Secretary of State, and as Vice President of the United States under two different presidents. The contemporary, colleague and sometime adversary of Daniel Webster and Henry Clay, Calhoun is widely regarded as one of the greatest senators in United States history.

Calhoun's son-in-law, Thomas Green Clemson, was cut from a different cloth. His marriage to Anna Maria Calhoun — on November 13, 1838, in the parlor at Fort Hill — was arguably one of the most important unions in South Carolina history.

Not a Southerner and never a politician, the Philadelphia-born Clemson was a man of science and the nation's first Superintendent of Agricultural Affairs. He was schooled in Europe because the kind of education he sought was not yet available in the United States. Perhaps it was as early as 1826, while attending lectures in chemistry at the Sorbonne, that Clemson conceived his vision of scientific education for America.

Whatever its origin, that vision gained immediacy and strength in the desperate poverty that was the aftermath of civil war. The state's cotton economy was bankrupt, her fields eroded and stripped of all nutrients. Clemson, one of the nation's leading experts on soil fertility and agricultural chemistry, knew, as he wrote in the late 1860's, "There is no hope for the South short of widespread scientific education."

That last, desperate hope led eventually to the institution we now call Clemson University.

It was founded after Thomas Clemson's death in 1888. His last will and testament called upon the State of South Carolina to accept his bequest of land (814 acres) and other assets (valued at about $80,000) to establish Clemson Agricultural College of South Carolina.

After court challenges to the will and a bitter floor fight in the state Legislature over its terms, the bequest was accepted. Clemson, the institution, dates its founding from November 27, 1889, when the Governor finally signed an Act of Acceptance establishing the college.

The early years were tough. Tight finances plagued the school during its construction and delayed its opening. Finally, on July 6, 1893, 446 cadets enrolled at the all-male, military institution.

With some modifications and despite four cadet "walkouts" between 1902 and 1924, the strict military administration prevailed for the next 60 years. Enrollment and curricula expanded slowly from the original emphasis on agriculture and "mechanics." Both the Depression and World War II took their toll, as enrollment dropped from 2,370 in 1942 to 745 in 1944. Like many schools, however, Clemson experienced a boom when the veterans began returning to classes in the late 1940's.

The graduate school was established in 1945, and a management study helped guide the way for the transition, in 1955, from a military to a civilian, co-educational institution. Women were admitted that year as full-time, degree-seeking students. In 1963, "integration with dignity" came to Clemson with the orderly enrollment of Harvey Gantt, Clemson's first black student.

Near disaster was averted when Lake Hartwell, completed in 1963, was built. The original plan would have flooded Memorial Stadium and thousands of acres of agricultural land acquired during the Depression. Under the leadership of then-Vice President R.C. Edwards, the Corps of Engineers added two dikes and a diversion channel, and the campus was saved.

In 1964, Clemson made the transition from college to university, when the Legislature formally recognized the expanded graduate offerings and research contributions.

The past is prologue

In 1989, Clemson University faces its second century with renewed pride, commitment and sense of purpose. Its almost 60,000 living alumni are making contributions in every walk of life. Its 14,000 students and 1,200 faculty members distinguish themselves in every field.

Not since its founding in 1893 has Clemson's mission to contribute to economic well-being and quality of life been more crucial to the future of South Carolina and the nation.

Under the leadership of President Max Lennon, a plan for excellence called "Clemson University: The Second Century" was developed two years ago. It provides a road map for Clemson into the 21st century, as it calls for renewed emphasis on teaching, research and public service programs in five broad areas:

- Agriculture and food
- Engineering and basic science
- Management and marketing
- Textiles, and those disciplines related to
- Quality of life

In the last five years alone, outside research support and private donations have more than doubled. More students than ever want to attend Clemson, and the quality of the student body continues to increase by any measure — high school standing, SAT scores, college achievement.

Plans are under way to expand the physical plant, last improved and enlarged in the late 1960's and early 70's, by adding facilities for biomedical and engineering research, performing arts, conferencing and continuing education, and recreation. Negotiations have begun to, literally, expand the campus worldwide.

Clemson University is proud of its past, but it does not live there. It is an institution that is clearly on the move, maturing and reaching toward its next plateau with an enthusiasm that is almost palpable.

Its outlook is reflected in the Centennial theme — Tradition and Vision. Anniversaries give us the opportunity to review where we've been, and to look forward to where we're headed.

As the next century approaches, you will see reflected in the pages of this volume an institution crackling with life, hope and vision for the future.

A CLEMSON CHRONOLOGY

1886 Thomas Green Clemson signs the final draft of his will leaving the bulk of his Fort Hill estate to the state to establish an agricultural college.

1888 Thomas Green Clemson dies on April 16, at 81 years old (today observed as Founder's Day); First meeting of the original seven Life Trustees takes place under an oak tree at Fort Hill as they plan to bring Clemson's dream to life.

1889 After a bitter debate and floor fight, the Act of Acceptance is passed by one vote and signed into law by Governor John P. Richardson. Clemson Agricultural College is now a reality.

1890 First meeting of Clemson's complete Board of Trustees at Wright's Hotel in Columbia; All 13 Trustees select Henry Aubrey Strode as Clemson's first president.

1891 Cornerstone of main building (Tillman Hall) is laid.

1893 Edwin Boone Craighead becomes Clemson's second president; 446 students enroll at the all-male military academy. School has 15 faculty.

1894 Main building (Tillman Hall) burns on May 22 when fire breaks out on the 3rd floor.

1895 Clemson's first degree is reported to have been awarded early to Charles Carter Newman (son of Professor J.S. Newman). Newman transferred to Clemson from Alabama Agricultural and Mechanical College (now Auburn University) and had a two-year head start on the other cadets.

1896 Clemson's first football team is organized and coached by future president Walter Merritt Riggs, an engineering teacher; Clemson plays its first football game against South Carolina College (now the University of South Carolina), losing 12 - 6; At Clemson's first commencement, 14 receive agricultural degrees, 18 receive mechanics degrees.

1897 Henry Simms Hartzog becomes Clemson's third president.

1900 Football legend John W. Heisman becomes coach at Clemson (1900-1903).

1902 Patrick Hues Mell becomes Clemson's fourth president.

1907 First issue of "The Tiger," the first college newspaper in South Carolina. Samuel R. Rhodes is the publication's first editor-in-chief.

1911 Walter Merritt Riggs becomes Clemson's fifth president.

1914 Clemson's first homecoming.

1915 The Cooperative Extension Service is established under the Smith-Lever Act. Lever, a co-author, is a South Carolina congressman and member of the Board.

1919 Albert Cleveland Corcoran composes Clemson's Alma Mater. Several decades later (in the 1950's), music teacher Hugh N. McGarity supplies the music still in use with Corcoran's lyrics today.

1925 Agriculture Hall (now Sikes Hall) burns; Enoch Walter Sikes becomes Clemson's sixth president.

1927 Clemson College becomes an accredited member of the Southern Association of Schools and Colleges.

1934 Professor George Aull (Class of 1919) begins a federal government project which eventually results in the acquisition of a little less than 30,000 acres by Clemson College. The land extends roughly seven miles north and south of the college; IPTAY formed.

1940 Robert Franklin Poole becomes Clemson's seventh president, and is the first Clemson alumnus to do so.

1957 Clemson graduates first female student — Margaret Marie Snider.

1959 Robert Cook Edwards becomes Clemson's eighth president.

1963 Harvey Gantt, Clemson's first black student, emrolls (He later becomes mayor of Charlotte, N.C.); Lucinda Brawley is first black woman to attend Clemson.

1964 Clemson Agricultural College becomes Clemson University.

1979 Bill Lee Atchley becomes Clemson's ninth president.

1982 Tigers beat Nebraska for first national football championship

1984 Clemson wins first national soccer championship.

1985 Walter Thompson Cox becomes Clemson's tenth president.

1986 Max Lennon becomes Clemson's eleventh president.

1987 Clemson wins its second national soccer title.

1988 Thomas Green Clemson inducted into the South Carolina Hall of Fame.

Outdoor Theatre and R.M. Cooper Library

A university may be a monument to its past, but the past must be served only in memory, not in performance. We believe that the investment of education is in the living, the young, the yet unborn. Though we are proud of Clemson University's accomplishments of the past, the true measure of our worth will be decided by our contribution to the future.

Clemson President Emeritus Robert Cook Edwards

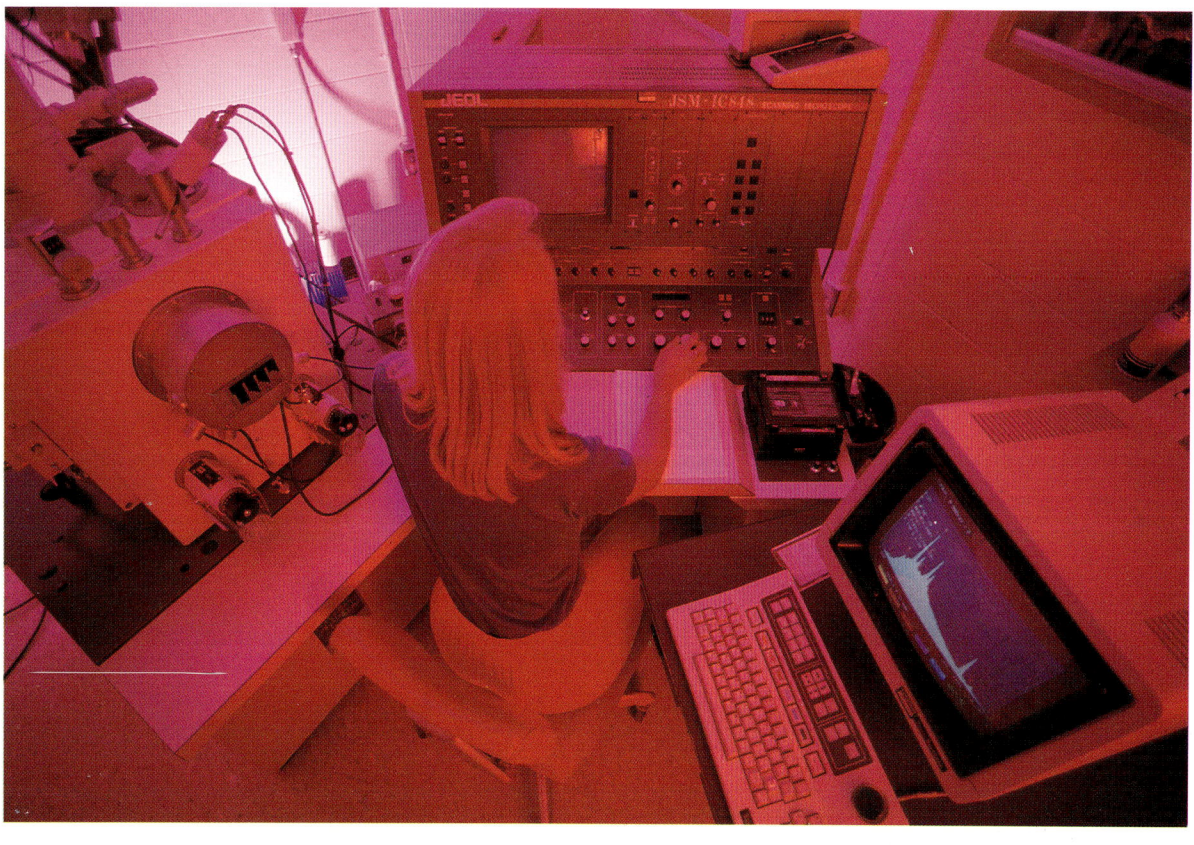

If you seek the real monument of Mr. Clemson, it is the steady and increasing stream of young people who have learned lessons of scholarship, education and service on Mr. Clemson's homeplace, Clemson University.

Clemson Vice Provost Jerry Reel, at Founders' Day banquet, 1986

Hardin Hall

Strode Tower from the Library

Clemson's former students have gone out from this institution with, I think, the finest education in the United States... I watch all of the schools and I don't believe there is a finer institution than Clemson... I say it because you have standards here that are extraordinarily high.

Charles L. Horn, president of the Olin Foundation

Biotechnology research

Lamaster Dairy Center

The most impressive aspect of Clemson University is not its campus, not even its highly sophisticated computers and exciting laboratories. It is a spirit that shines in the faces and resounds above the words of Clemson staff and faculty people as they talk about what they are doing and what they hope to do. That is what really makes a university, and Clemson has it.

The Greenville News, April, 1969

Fort Hill, the Calhoun Home

Mr. Clemson often looked over to where the college now stands and said, "That's the place for the institution. I want it to be a school for teaching every farm and city boy in South Carolina."

Mrs. Jane Prince, housekeeper to Thomas Clemson, in 1940

As the lake finally came into being, more people were pleased than displeased. The scenery certainly was improved. The view from the top of the Clemson House, with stretches of blue water against a backdrop of green hills and, further away, mountains, became spectacular.

Wright Bryan in *Clemson: An Informal History of the University*

Lake Hartwell

Mother Nature made it beautiful with gently undulating hill and dale; with umbrageous forest growth skillfully manipulated, making the handsomest specimen of landscape gardening in the state.

J.E. Norment in *The Darlington News and Press*, May, 1933

Botanical Garden

R. M. Cooper Library

I am grateful for the important contributions which Clemson made to my life, and I am very proud of Clemson University today. Clemson has become not only an institution of academic excellence in many fields; it is not only known throughout the country for the quality of basic and applied research conducted by scientists and graduate students; it is also a great public service institution, extending the benefits of academic knowledge and research discoveries to citizens throughout our state and the nation.

Senator Strom Thurmond, address at Clemson, October 1981

To no one factor can the rejuvenation of South Carolina in the past century be attributed. Hundreds of institutions, thousands of individuals, many sweeping forces, including general economic growth of the nation, have contributed to the happy result. But beyond dispute, the training, the research, and public services provided by Clemson College and Clemson University, especially in years before other institutions and forces had come fully into play, constitute a major factor in creating the South Carolina of today. Some, with the pride of loyal sons, would say Clemson was the major factor, and remains so today.

Wright Bryan in *Clemson: An Informal History of the University*

Hunter Chemistry Laboratory

Sirrine Hall

Riggs Hall

Riggs Hall

50

Clemson Memorial Carillon

Sirrine Hall

Downtown Clemson

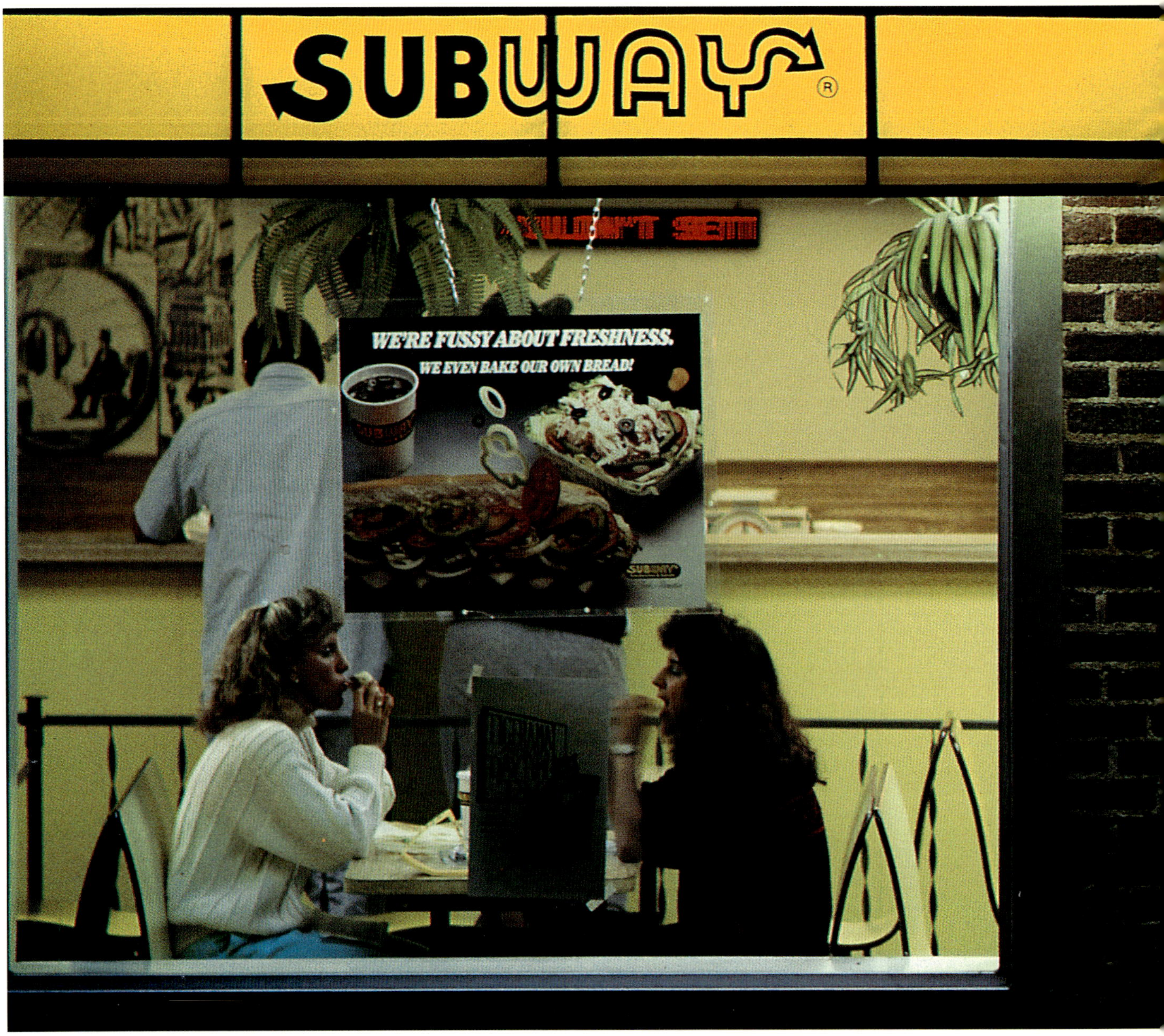
SUBWAY
WE'RE FUSSY ABOUT FRESHNESS.
WE EVEN BAKE OUR OWN BREAD!

SHERWIN-WILLIAMS
PAINTS
JUDGE KELLER
GENERAL MERCHANDISE
367
MENS
HARDWA

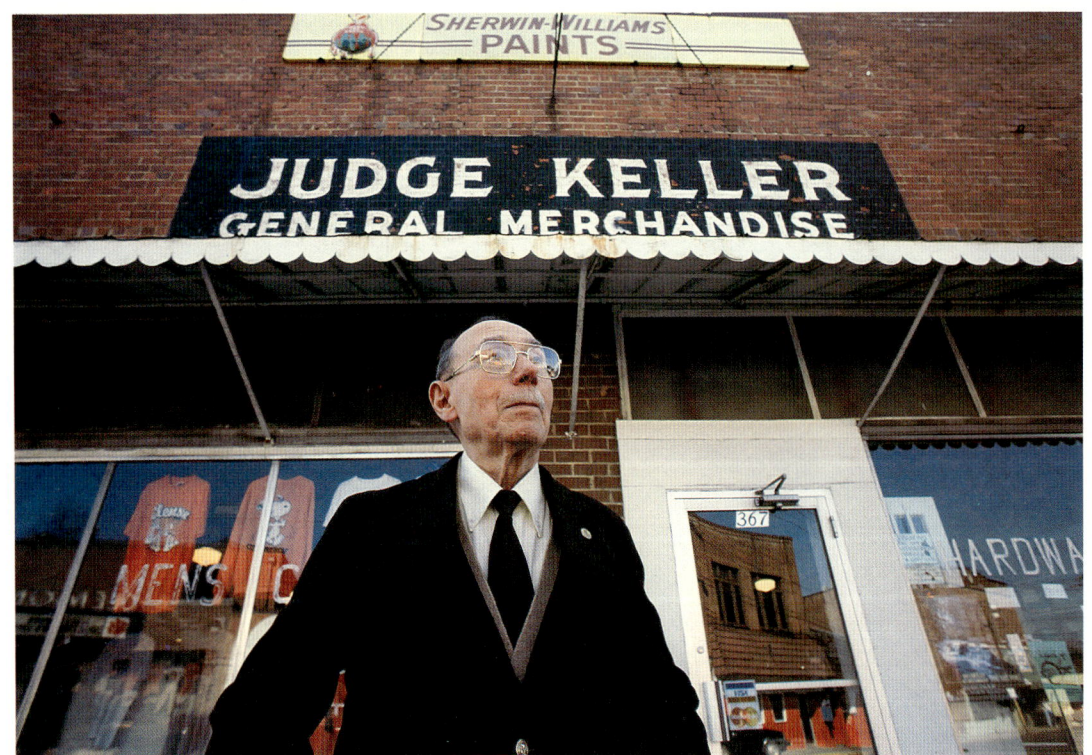

Esso Club

Edgar A. Brown University Union

Fraternity Hall

Johnstone Hall

There's something in these hills that has touched anyone who has been associated with Clemson, something that has rubbed off on them in varying degrees, something that has built within the breast of all Clemson men and women an enduring spark akin to an eternal pride.

Joe Sherman in *There's Something in These Hills*

60

Fraternity Quad

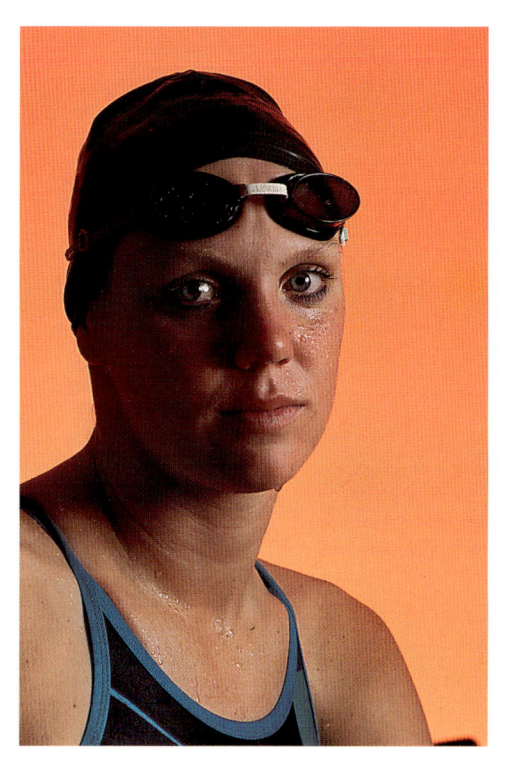

SAT MORN PRACTICE CANCELLED
Royal Fireworks
"A CHORUS LINE"
FESTIQUE
AT THE BALLET

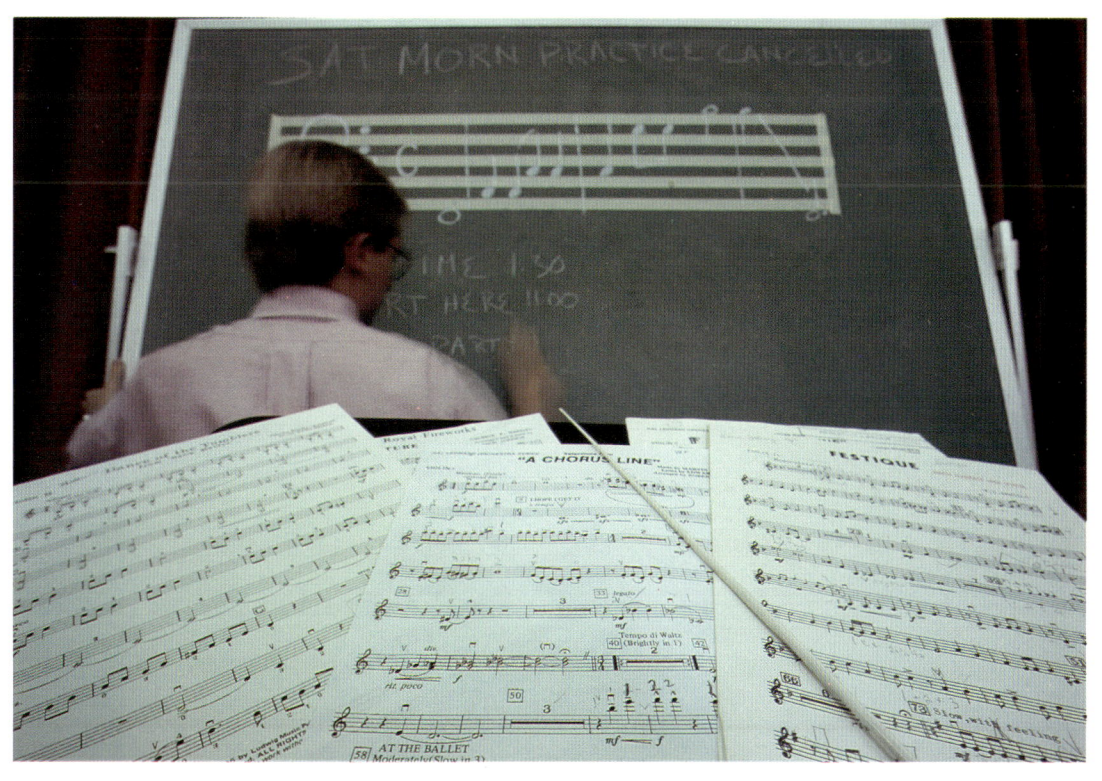

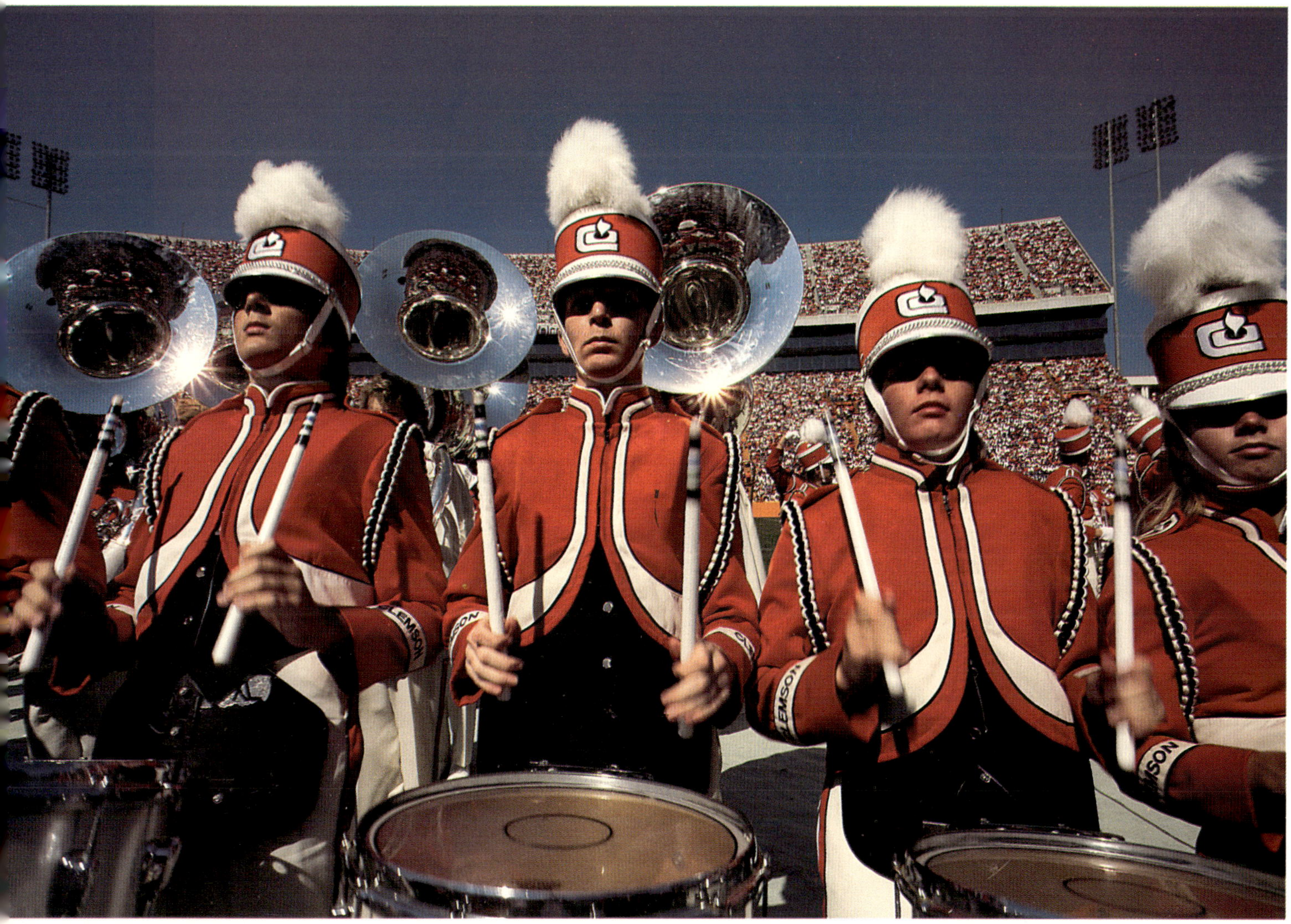

In the hearts of most folk who experience Clemson, a desire is engendered to return to Tigertown or recall life there. Clemson is sacred ground. Good humor has eased anxious times; the friendliness of Clemson folk has built lasting connections.

Mary Catherine Littlejohn in *Tales of Tigertown*, 1979

Clemson Memorial Stadium and Frank Howard Field

Coach Frank Howard

Despite my Furman background, I grew up with a deep respect for opposing Clemson, which ceased to be an opponent many years ago because of the people there who became friends. And as the friends grew, so did the respect. A father can only measure the people of an athletic administration by one rule of the heart; would you like your son to be playing for them? I would like my own son to be playing for Clemson. To be a Tiger.

Furman Bisher in the *Atlanta Journal*

The members of the General Assembly, by this resolution, would like to recognize and commend every member of the staff and crew of The Clemson Players for their truly outstanding drama and theater success which has brought much deserved recognition not only to The Clemson Players and Clemson University but to the State of South Carolina as well.

Resolution of the South Carolina General Assembly, 1984

87

Clemson College is not a college merely — it is a great public service corporation, whose worth must be measured by the total of the service it renders. Through its research, regulatory and extension work and other public activities, the college campus has been extended to include the entire state. The institution has indeed become the fireside university of our agricultural people.

Clemson President W.M. Riggs, in *The Greenville News*, December 3, 1923

90

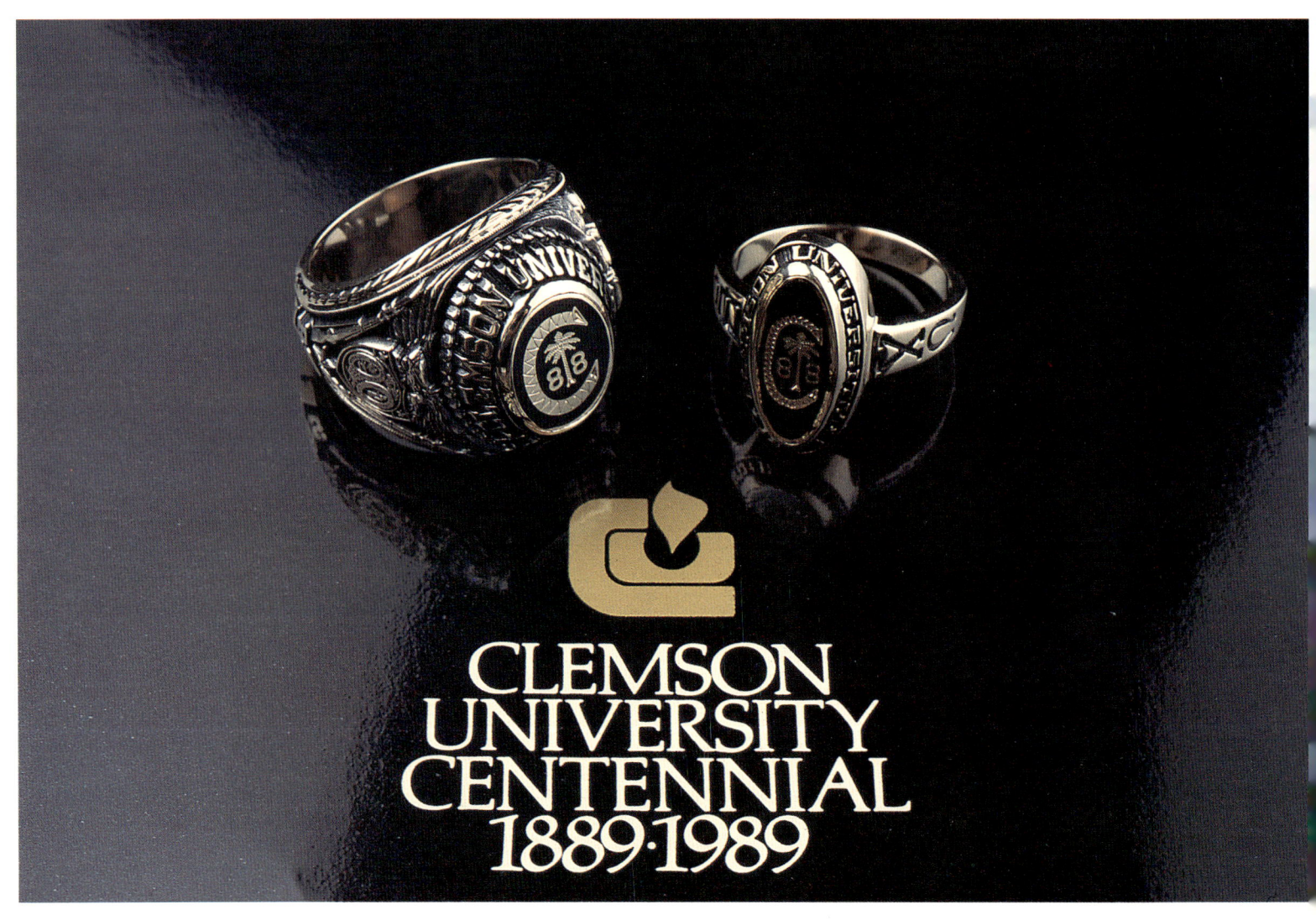

A LOOK BACK AT CLEMSON

A SELECTION OF PHOTOS FROM THE 60's, 70's and 80's

Look for the definitive photographic history of Clemson in the upcoming book *Visions : Clemson's Yesteryears*, available in November, 1989.

CLEMSON PEOPLE

President and Mrs. R.C. Edwards at the Robert Cook Edwards Day Salute, May 11, 1979.

Senator Strom Thurmond and Vice President George Bush wield the shovels at the Strom Thurmond Institute groundbreaking ceremony. In the background, from left, are Clemson University President Walter T. Cox, Strom Thurmond II, Paul Thurmond and Nancy Thurmond.

At right: Clemson football coach Danny Ford became the youngest coach ever to win the national football championship and to be named national coach of the year in 1981.

Below: Former Clemson student Shawn Weatherly, 1977 Miss Homecoming and 1980 Miss Universe, returned to campus for a visit during her reign in 1980, taking part in the First Friday Parade.

Frank Howard was on the Clemson staff for 43 years, including 30 as head coach, during which time he won 165 games. Howard is nationally known not only for his football success, but also for his after-dinner forays around the country.

CLEMSON PEOPLE

Walter Cox, Clemson University's 10th president and most beloved dean, receives congratulations from James C. Hambright, Jr. of Rock Hill, South Carolina, at a salute given to Dean Cox upon his retirement in 1987.

Bill Atchley, Clemson University's ninth president (1979-1985) with Faculty Senate President Stassen Thompson.

Marking the beginning of Clemson's desegregation period, Harvey Gantt became the University's first black student on January 28, 1963. Gantt was an architecture major at Clemson, and went on to become a successful businessman and mayor of Charlotte, North Carolina.

Opera star Beverly Sills visits Clemson, April 11, 1988. She was the central speaker for the first segment of the Clemson Centennial observance. With her are Dr. Jerome Reel (left), the driving force of the Centennial celebration, and the University's president, Dr. Max Lennon.

CLEMSON GROWTH

South stands upper deck of Clemson Memorial Stadium; completed in 1978.

The R. M. Cooper Library; completed in 1979.

The Pee Dee Research and Education Center, Florence, South Carolina; completed in 1984.

The University Union; completed in 1975

Byrnes Hall; completed in 1970.

Jordan Hall; completed in 1976.

Daniel Hall; completed in 1968.

CLEMSON GROWTH

The 1960's and 1970's were years of tremendous growth for Clemson. This airview from about 1980 shows the development of campus buildings and facilities.

Smith Hall; completed 1973.

Rhodes Engineering Research Center; completed 1969.

The Nursing Building; completed 1978.

CLEMSON MILESTONES

Women became part of the Clemson environment September 7, 1955, as the University became coeducational. Mary Olis Brooks, (left), studied horticulture and received her B.S. degree in 1967.

In 1984 all six of Clemson's nominated students won Fulbright scholarships to study in Europe, a feat matched by no other university. Kathryn Cole (left) and Nancy Snow were part of that group.

Sally Hester and William Jones received two of the first diplomas granted at commencement, 1964, after Clemson College became Clemson University.

The Ampitheater crowd at commencement in 1966 witnessed the conferring of degrees for the first time with the Robert M. Cooper Library as the building/backdrop/ for the ceremony.

The A. Wolfe Davidson statue of Thomas Green Clemson, prior to being bronzed in 1966.

Clemson University Extension Service Director Johnny Brewer (right) advises a soybean grower on soil and plant conditions. The Clemson Extension Service has an office in every county in South Carolina.

Mandatory ROTC training was a Clemson tradition for many years. The officer training program became elective in 1970.

CLEMSON STUDENT LIFE

The toga pep rally.

Fraternity tug-of-war, Greek Week 1984.

The brothers of Sigma Phi Epsilon each year paint the Tiger paws on the roads leading to Clemson.

Graham Frye, Michael Tierney and Robin Roberts perform in a scene from *American Buffalo*. The 1984 Clemson Players production received national recognition when invited to participate in the American College Theater Festival at the Kennedy Center in Washington, D.C.

Students sitting on the Tillman Auditorium stage fill out the computer cards needed to register for classes.

Jane Fonda visited Clemson and talked to the student body in the ampitheater in 1970.

The famous Clemson spirit became world-class on November 12, 1983, when Clemson fans set a world record by releasing 363, 729 balloons at the Clemson-Maryland game. (Clemson won 52-27).

Clemson does get an occasional snow despite a generally pleasant climate, and Clemson students know how to have a good time in it.

First Friday Parades began in 1974 and have become a Clemson tradition. This group marches through downtown Clemson the day before the 1981 Clemson-Georgia football game.

Students prepare to dig into one of the world's largest banana splits, a 400-foot-long masterpiece prepared by the Student Union in 1973 as part of "November Nonsense."

CLEMSON ATHLETICS

Noel Loban, Clemson's NCAA wrestling champion in the 190-pound class in 1980, defeats a Virginia wrestler in this match in Jervey Athletic Center. In his three years at Clemson, Loban compiled an 88-13 record.

One of many memorable plays in Clemson's football history was this game-winning touchdown pass from Steve Fuller to Jerry Butler in the 1977 Clemson-South Carolina game. The Tigers defeated the Gamecocks 27-24, and won a berth in the 1977 Gator Bowl.

The NCAA champion Clemson soccer team, under coach I.M. Ibrahim, takes a victory lap after winning the title at the Seattle Kingdome in 1984. Clemson won another title in 1987.

Barbara Kennedy is the Lady Tigers all-time leading scorer and rebounder. She is the first and only Clemson female athlete to have her number retired, and the only female athlete to be named IPTAY Athlete-of-the-Year.

Battling for a spot in the 1958 College World Series, the Tigers faced certain defeat, down 10-3 to the Florida nine with four innings to play. The Tigers staged a memorable comeback, however, defeating the Gators 15-14, then beat them again 3-1 to earn the World Series bid.

Clemson's only trip to the finals of the Atlantic Coast Conference Tournament came in 1962 when the Tigers upset N.C. State and Duke. Here the jubilant Tigers celebrate the 75-72 win over Duke. Clemson's Jim Brennan scored 34 points.

After winning the national football championship in 1981, President Reagan invited members of the team to the White House. Quarterback Homer Jordan, far left, and wide receiver Jerry Gaillard, second from left, presented the president with a Clemson T-shirt. On the right is South Carolina's senior senator Strom Thurmond, and Deborah Ford, wife of Clemson head coach Danny Ford.